ADORNMENTS OF INDIA

A JOURNEY THROUGH THE HISTORY AND ARTISTRY BEHIND INDIAN JEWELRY

DR. JAGADEESH PILLAI

Copyright © Dr. Jagadeesh Pillai
All Rights Reserved.

This book has been self-published with all reasonable efforts taken to make the material error-free by the author. No part of this book shall be used, reproduced in any manner whatsoever without written permission from the author, except in the case of brief quotations embodied in critical articles and reviews.

The Author of this book is solely responsible and liable for its content including but not limited to the views, representations, descriptions, statements, information, opinions and references ["Content"]. The Content of this book shall not constitute or be construed or deemed to reflect the opinion or expression of the Publisher or Editor. Neither the Publisher nor Editor endorse or approve the Content of this book or guarantee the reliability, accuracy or completeness of the Content published herein and do not make any representations or warranties of any kind, express or implied, including but not limited to the implied warranties of merchantability, fitness for a particular purpose. The Publisher and Editor shall not be liable whatsoever for any errors, omissions, whether such errors or omissions result from negligence, accident, or any other cause or claims for loss or damages of any kind, including without limitation, indirect or consequential loss or damage arising out of use, inability to use, or about the reliability, accuracy or sufficiency of the information contained in this book.

Made with ♥ on the Notion Press Platform
www.notionpress.com

|| Dedicated to all wisdom seekers around the World ||

॥ॐ॥

Contents

Contents

Prayer

**"Om Bhadram Karnebhih Shrunuyaama
DevaahBhadram Pashyemaakshabhiryajatraah
SthirairangaistushtuvaamsastanoobhihVyashema
Devahitam YadaayuhSwasti Na Indro
VridhashravaahSwasti Nah Pooshaa
VishwavedaahSwasti Nastaarkshyo ArishtanemihSwasti
No Brihaspatir DadhaatuOm Shantih, Shantih, Shantih"**

The literal meaning of this mantra is: OM. O Gods! Let us
hear auspicious words from our ears. O reverent Gods! Let
us behold propitious visions from our eyes, let our organs
and body be stable, healthy, and strong. Let us do that
which is pleasing to the gods in the life span allotted to us.
May Indra, inscribed in the scriptures, bring us fortune!
May Pushan, the knower of the world, grant us prosperity!
May Trakshya, who vanquishes enemies, bestow us with
blessings! May Brihaspati bring us success!
OM Peace, Peace, Peace.

About The Author

Dr. Jagadeesh Pillai is a renowned Guinness World Record holder, writer, and researcher hailing from Varanasi, also known as the abode of Lord Shiva. With a Ph.D. in Vedic Science and a range of creative ideas and achievements, he is a true polymath. He is the author of more than 100 books including Research Publications. Although his roots can be traced back to Kerala, the people of Varanasi hold him in high regard and affectionately consider him one of their own.

In 1998, Dr. Pillai was offered a job at Banaras Hindu University, but he left the position after only two months to pursue greater goals in life. He believed that in order to study Indian scriptures and engage in other creative endeavours, he needed to retire from the daily grind of working solely for money at a young age.

He started an export business from scratch, using the knowledge he had gained from a previous job in the industry. His intelligence and unique approach to business led to great success in a short period of time, earning him more in just a decade and a half than he would have in a lifetime working in a government job. Upon the passing of Dr. APJ Abdul Kalam, Dr. Pillai decided to leave the business and dedicate himself to reading, studying, researching, and experimenting.

During his tenure in the export business, Dr. Pillai traveled to over 16 countries, gaining valuable insight and experiencing the world and life in detail.

Dr. Pillai has achieved four Guinness World Records in the following subjects:

"Script to Screen" - In this record, Dr. Pillai produced and directed an animation film within the shortest time possible, breaking the previous record set by Canadians. He has also received numerous national and international awards and recognitions for this achievement.

Longest Line of Postcards - For this record, Dr. Pillai created a line of 16,300 postcards on the occasion of the 163rd anniversary of Indian Postal Day. The event also included a questionnaire about the Indian flag.

Largest Poster Awareness Campaign - Dr. Pillai designed an awareness campaign on the subject of "Beti Bachao - Beti Padhao" (Save the Girl Child - Educate the Girl Child) to achieve this record.

Largest Envelope - In tribute to the Indian Prime Minister's "Make in India" initiative, Dr. Pillai created a 4000 square meter envelope using waste paper to achieve this record.

Attempted - **70000 Candles on a 210 kg Cake** - To celebrate the 70th Indian Independence Day, Dr. Pillai attempted to light 70,000 candles on a 210 kg cake, which was recorded in World Records India.

Attempted - **Documentary on Dhamek Stupa of Sarnath in 17 Languages** - Dr. Pillai attempted to create a documentary on the Dhamek Stupa of Sarnath, dubbing it in 17 different languages. The result of this attempt is currently awaiting confirmation from the Guinness World Records.

Dr. Pillai is skilled in teaching the Bhagavad Gita, a Hindu scripture, and is popular among young people. He has helped many young people improve their lives through his motivational teachings.

In addition to teaching, he has composed and sung numerous Sanskrit Bhajans and patriotic songs.

He has also written and directed several short films and documentaries for awareness campaigns, and has volunteered with the police in both UP and Kerala to spread awareness about various issues through videos and photography.

Incredibly, he has produced and directed over 100 documentaries about the city of Varanasi, all on his own.

He has also helped and guided more than 25 boys and girls to achieve world records through creative and innovative methods. He is a multifaceted person who uses his intellect and the blessings given to him by God to excel in various areas. He is both a teacher and a student, always learning and teaching, and is able to master any subject he comes across.

He is a selfless social activist and motivational speaker who has overcome struggles and failures to become a successful and enthusiastic individual with a rich life experience.

In addition to his work with the Bhagavad Gita, he is also an efficient Tarot card reader, Astro-Vastu consultant, and a talented singer and composer. He has sung the entire Ram Charita Manas and Bhagavad Gita in his own compositions, and has sung the phrase "Lokah Samastha Sukhino Bhavantu" in 50 different languages. He is currently working on a detailed and scientific study of Vedas, Upanishads, Puranas, and the Bhagavad Gita. He has also composed and sung the Hanuman Chalisa and Gayatri Mantra in 108 and 1008 different compositions, respectively.

Awards - Four Times Guinness World Records, Winner of Mahatma Gandhi Vishwa Shanti Puraskar, Mahatma Gandhi Global Peace Ambassador, Kashi Ratna Award, Dr. APJ Abdul Kalam Motivational Person of the Year 2017, Mother Teresa Award, Indira Gandhi Priyadarshini Award, Bharat Vikas Ratna Award, Udyog Ratna Award, Vigyan Prasar Award, Poorvanchal Ratn Samman.

Preface

Jewelry has been a significant adornment for Indian women since ages. Its significance in an Indian woman's life can be judged from the number of jewelry gifts she receives on a variety of auspicious occasions in her life and how even the poorest of women possess some kind of jewelry they can afford. Indian women's decorating themselves with jewelry is not only a customary tradition, but also has a lot of values attached to each and every jewelry piece worn by the women.

My goal for this book, The Indian Jewelry: A Look into the History and Significance of Indian Jewelry Making, is to explore the history and significance of Indian jewelry and the many ways in which it has shaped Indian culture and society. This book is intended to serve as an introduction to the rich history and culture of Indian jewelry for readers who are new to the subject. It explores the evolution of Indian jewelry from its traditional roots to its modern-day forms. The book covers various topics, including the development of different jewelry styles, the emergence of popular jewelry designers, and the impact of Indian jewelry on the global market. It also examines the economics of the Indian jewelry industry and explores how technological and societal changes have shaped its evolution.

The book draws on research from a variety of sources, including interviews with key figures in the Indian jewelry industry, archival materials, and cultural analysis. I have also conducted extensive field research in India, including attending jewelry shows, interviewing jewelry designers, and visiting locations associated with the production of Indian jewelry. Through this research, I hope to provide readers with a comprehensive understanding of the Indian jewelry industry and its various components.

I believe that Indian jewelry has a great deal to offer to the world and I am excited to share its cultural and historical significance with.

Indian Traditional Necklace

I

Introduction to Indian Jewelry

India has a rich and diverse cultural heritage, reflected in its traditional arts and crafts, one of which is jewelry. Indian jewelry has a long history, stretching back to ancient times, and has been an important part of the country's cultural identity for centuries. From simple beaded necklaces to elaborate gold bracelets and necklaces, Indian jewelry is characterized by its intricate designs, intricate workmanship, and use of precious and semi-precious stones.

The history of Indian jewelry can be traced back to the Indus Valley Civilization, which flourished around 2500 BC. During this period, the people of the Indus Valley were skilled in metalworking, and they produced intricate jewelry pieces made of gold, silver, and other metals. With the arrival of the Mughals in the 16th century, Indian jewelry became even more intricate and sophisticated, with the use of precious and semi-precious stones such as diamonds, rubies, emeralds, and pearls becoming more widespread.

Indian jewelry is known for its diverse styles and designs, reflecting the country's different regions, cultures, and religions. The northern regions of India, for example, are known for their traditional Kundan jewelry, which is made from gold and features intricate designs, while the southern regions are known for their temple jewelry, which is made from silver and is often decorated with colorful stones.

One of the most distinctive features of Indian jewelry is its use of intricate designs and detailed workmanship. Many pieces of Indian jewelry are handcrafted by skilled artisans, who use techniques such as enameling, engraving, and filigree to create intricate patterns and designs. In addition to the intricate designs, Indian jewelry is also known for its use of precious and semi-precious stones, such as diamonds, rubies, emeralds, and pearls, which are set into the pieces to create a striking and eye-catching effect.

Another unique aspect of Indian jewelry is its versatility. Indian jewelry can be worn on a daily basis or reserved for special occasions, such as weddings and festivals. Indian women, in particular, have a love for jewelry and often wear multiple pieces at the same time, including earrings, necklaces, bracelets, and bangles. This is a reflection of the importance of jewelry in Indian culture, as it is seen not only as a fashion accessory but also as a symbol of wealth, status, and beauty.

Indian jewelry is a rich and diverse art form that reflects the country's long history and cultural heritage. From its intricate designs and workmanship to its use of precious and semi-precious stones, Indian jewelry is a true testament to the talent and skill of the country's artisans and a celebration of the beauty and diversity of India's cultural heritage. Whether you are an admirer of jewelry or simply interested in learning more about the rich history and artistry behind Indian jewelry, "Adornments of India: A Journey Through the History and Artistry Behind Indian Jewelry" will take you on an unforgettable journey through the fascinating world of Indian jewelry.

"Jewelry has always been more than just adornment in India, it is a reflection of the country's rich history and cultural heritage."

৪৩

II

History of Indian Jewelry Making

Indian jewelry has a rich and diverse history that stretches back thousands of years, with evidence of jewelry making dating back to the Indus Valley Civilization of the 3rd millennium BCE. During this time, the people of the Indus Valley were skilled in metalworking and produced intricate jewelry pieces made of gold, silver, and other metals. These early pieces of jewelry were not just functional but also held religious and cultural significance.

With the arrival of the Mughal Empire in the 16th century, Indian jewelry making reached new heights of sophistication and intricate workmanship. The Mughals brought with them new techniques, such as enameling, and a love for precious stones, which were incorporated into Indian jewelry designs. During this period, Indian jewelry became known for its intricate designs, intricate workmanship, and use of precious and semi-precious stones, and it was highly prized both within India and abroad.

One of the most distinctive features of Indian jewelry making is the use of traditional techniques, many of which have been passed down from generation to generation. These techniques include enameling, engraving, filigree, and Meenakari, a traditional form of enameling that involves painting designs onto metal surfaces and then heating them to create a permanent finish. Indian jewelry makers also use a wide range of materials, including gold, silver, brass, and copper, and often incorporate precious and semi-precious stones such as diamonds, rubies, emeralds, and pearls into their designs.

The different regions of India also have their own unique styles of jewelry making, reflecting the cultural and religious differences of each area. For example, the northern regions of India are known for their traditional Kundan jewelry, which is made from gold and features intricate designs, while the southern regions are known for their temple jewelry, which is made from silver and is often decorated with colorful stones.

The art of jewelry making in India has not remained static but has evolved over the centuries, reflecting changes in cultural and economic circumstances. In the 20th century, for example, the Indian independence movement and the subsequent establishment of the Republic of India led to a renewed interest in traditional Indian arts and crafts, including jewelry making. Today, Indian jewelry making continues to thrive, with artisans and designers exploring new techniques and materials while also preserving the traditional skills and methods passed down through generations.

The history of Indian jewelry making is a rich and diverse story that spans thousands of years and reflects the country's cultural, religious, and economic heritage. From the ancient Indus Valley Civilization to the arrival of the Mughals, and from the independence movement to the modern era, Indian jewelry making has always been a celebration of the beauty and diversity of India's cultural heritage. Whether you are a collector of jewelry, an admirer of traditional arts and crafts, or simply interested in learning more about the rich history and artistry behind Indian jewelry, "Adornments of India: A Journey Through the History and Artistry Behind Indian Jewelry" will take you on a fascinating journey through the world of Indian jewelry making.

"The legacy of Indian jewelry is a story woven with intricate designs, precious stones, and techniques passed down through generations."

৪৩

III

Types of Indian Jewelry

Indian jewelry is renowned for its diversity and beauty, and there are countless different styles and designs to choose from. Whether you are looking for traditional jewelry, contemporary pieces, or something in between, there is an Indian jewelry style to suit every taste and occasion. In this chapter, we will explore some of the most popular and distinctive types of Indian jewelry, including:

Kundan Jewelry:

Kundan is a traditional form of jewelry making that originated in northern India. Kundan jewelry is typically made from gold and features intricate designs that are created using small pieces of metal that are carefully shaped and molded to fit together. Kundan jewelry is typically set with precious and semi-precious stones, including diamonds, rubies, emeralds, and pearls.

Meenakari Jewelry:

Meenakari is a traditional form of enameling that is often used in Indian jewelry making. This technique involves painting designs onto metal surfaces and then heating them to create a permanent finish. Meenakari jewelry is often characterized by its vibrant, colorful designs and intricate patterns, and it is highly prized for its beauty and craftsmanship.

Temple Jewelry:

Temple jewelry is a type of jewelry that originated in southern India and is often associated with Hindu temple worship. Temple jewelry is typically made from silver and is often decorated with colorful stones, such as rubies, emeralds, and sapphires. The designs of temple jewelry are often inspired by religious symbols and motifs, such as deities, flowers, and animals.

Jadau Jewelry:

Jadau is a traditional form of jewelry making that is associated with the Indian state of Rajasthan. Jadau jewelry is made from gold and features intricate designs that are created using small pieces of metal that are carefully shaped and molded to fit together. Jadau jewelry is often set with precious and semi-precious stones, including diamonds, rubies, and emeralds, and is prized for its beauty and craftsmanship.

Antique Jewelry:

Antique jewelry is a term used to describe jewelry that is more than 100 years old. Antique jewelry can be made from any material and can take many different forms, from traditional Kundan and Meenakari jewelry to more modern styles. Antique jewelry is highly prized for its rarity, beauty, and historical significance, and it is often sought after by collectors and admirers of traditional Indian jewelry.

Contemporary Jewelry:

Contemporary jewelry refers to jewelry that is made using modern techniques and materials, and that reflects contemporary design trends and styles. Contemporary jewelry can take many different forms, from simple and minimalist pieces to more elaborate and intricate designs.

Whether you are looking for traditional Kundan jewelry, vibrant Meenakari pieces, intricate temple jewelry, or contemporary designs, Indian jewelry offers something for everyone. Whether you are a collector, an admirer of traditional arts and crafts, or simply looking for a beautiful piece of jewelry to wear, "Adornments of India: A Journey Through the History and Artistry Behind Indian Jewelry" is an essential guide to the world of Indian jewelry, exploring the beauty, craftsmanship, and cultural significance of this diverse and captivating art form.

"Indian jewelry is a symphony of colors, a
fusion of styles, and a testament to the
country's enduring artistic traditions."

❦

IV
Traditional Jewelry Making Techniques

Indian jewelry is renowned for its intricate designs, beautiful craftsmanship, and cultural significance, and much of this can be attributed to the traditional jewelry making techniques that have been passed down through generations. In this chapter, we will explore some of the most important and distinctive traditional jewelry making techniques that are used in India, including:

Kundan:

Kundan is a traditional form of jewelry making that originated in northern India. Kundan jewelry is typically made from gold and features intricate designs that are created using small pieces of metal that are carefully shaped and molded to fit together. Kundan jewelry is often set with precious and semi-precious stones, including diamonds, rubies, emeralds, and pearls, and is prized for its beauty and craftsmanship.

Meenakari:

Meenakari is a traditional form of enameling that is often used in Indian jewelry making. This technique involves painting designs onto metal surfaces and then heating them to create a permanent finish. Meenakari jewelry is often characterized by its vibrant, colorful designs and intricate patterns, and it is highly prized for its beauty and craftsmanship.

Filigree:

Filigree is a traditional form of jewelry making that involves creating intricate designs by twisting and braiding thin wires of gold or silver. Filigree jewelry is often characterized by its delicate and lacy appearance, and it is highly prized for its beauty and craftsmanship.

Chasing and Repoussé:

Chasing and Repoussé are traditional jewelry making techniques that involve shaping metal by hammering it from the front and back. This allows for intricate designs and shapes to be created, and is often used to create detailed images and patterns on jewelry.

Engraving:

Engraving is a traditional jewelry making technique that involves carving designs into the surface of metal using specialized tools. Engraving can be used to create intricate patterns and designs, and is often used in combination with other techniques, such as filigree, chasing and repoussé, to create truly unique and beautiful pieces of jewelry.

Stone Setting:

Stone setting is an important jewelry making technique that involves attaching gems and other precious stones to jewelry using prongs, claws, or other methods. Stone setting can be used to create intricate and elaborate designs, and is often used in combination with other techniques, such as filigree and engraving, to create truly beautiful and unique pieces of jewelry.

These traditional jewelry making techniques have been passed down through generations in India, and are still used today by artisans and craftsmen to create beautiful and intricate pieces of jewelry. Whether you are a collector, an admirer of traditional arts and crafts, or simply looking for a beautiful piece of jewelry to wear, "Adornments of India: A Journey Through the History and Artistry Behind Indian Jewelry" is an essential guide to the world of Indian jewelry, exploring the beauty, craftsmanship, and cultural significance of this diverse and captivating art form.

"From the ancient Indus Valley Civilization to the present day, Indian jewelry has been a symbol of beauty, power, and spiritual significance."

৪১

Indian Traditional Jewelry

V

Popular Jewelry Styles in India

India is a land of diverse cultures and traditions, and this is reflected in the wide variety of jewelry styles that are popular across the country. From traditional styles that have been passed down through generations, to contemporary designs that are influenced by modern fashion trends, Indian jewelry is both beautiful and diverse. In this chapter, we will explore some of the most popular jewelry styles in India, including:

Nath:

The Nath is a traditional nose ring that is popular in India. This jewelry style is often made from gold or silver and features intricate designs and embellishments. The Nath is an important part of traditional Indian bridal jewelry and is often worn by women on their wedding day.

Jhumka:

The Jhumka is a traditional earring style that is popular in India. This jewelry style is typically made from gold or silver and features a bell-shaped design with intricate embellishments. Jhumkas are often worn with traditional Indian clothing and are an important part of traditional Indian bridal jewelry.

Choker:

The Choker is a popular neck jewelry style that is commonly worn in India. This jewelry style is typically made from gold or silver and features a close-fitting design that sits high on the neck. Chokers can be simple and elegant or elaborate and ornate, and are often worn with traditional Indian clothing.

Anklet:

The Anklet is a popular jewelry style that is worn around the ankle. This jewelry style is often made from gold or silver and features intricate designs and embellishments. Anklets are an important part of traditional Indian bridal jewelry and are often worn by women on their wedding day.

Bangles:

Bangles are a popular jewelry style that is worn around the wrist. This jewelry style is often made from gold or silver and can be simple and elegant or elaborate and ornate. Bangles are a staple of traditional Indian jewelry and are often worn in sets of multiple bangles on each wrist.

Maang Tikka:

The Maang Tikka is a traditional hair accessory that is popular in India. This jewelry style is typically made from gold or silver and features a long chain with a pendant that is worn in the hair. Maang Tikkas are an important part of traditional Indian bridal jewelry and are often worn by women on their wedding day.

Toe Rings:

Toe Rings are a popular jewelry style that is worn on the toes. This jewelry style is often made from gold or silver and can be simple and elegant or elaborate and ornate. Toe rings are an important part of traditional Indian bridal jewelry and are often worn by women on their wedding day.

These popular jewelry styles are just a few examples of the diverse and beautiful jewelry that is made and worn in India. Whether you are looking for a traditional piece of jewelry to wear with traditional Indian clothing, or a contemporary design to wear with modern outfits, there is a wealth of jewelry styles to choose from in India. "Adornments of India: A Journey Through the History and Artistry Behind Indian Jewelry" is an essential guide to the world of Indian jewelry, exploring the beauty, craftsmanship, and cultural significance of this diverse and captivating art form.

"The art of jewelry making in India has been influenced by numerous cultures, each leaving their unique mark on the country's rich heritage."

VI

The Economics of Indian Jewelry

The jewelry industry is a major contributor to the economy of India, with a rich history and tradition of craftsmanship and design. From the creation of intricate gold and silver pieces to the production of precious gemstones, the Indian jewelry industry has played a significant role in the growth and development of the country for centuries. In this chapter, we will explore the economics of Indian jewelry, including:

Production:

The production of jewelry in India is a complex and multi-faceted process that involves the creation of designs, the sourcing of materials, and the crafting of pieces. The industry is comprised of a wide range of small and large-scale manufacturers, including family-owned businesses, co-operatives, and multinational corporations.

Exportation:

India is one of the largest exporters of jewelry in the world, with a significant portion of its production being sold to international markets. The country's jewelry industry is well-established and has a reputation for quality and craftsmanship, making it a popular choice for consumers around the world.

Domestic Market:

The domestic market for jewelry in India is also significant, with a large portion of the population buying and wearing jewelry for both personal and cultural reasons. Jewelry is an important part of many Indian celebrations and ceremonies, including weddings, and is often given as gifts to commemorate special events and milestones.

Labor and Employment:

The jewelry industry in India provides employment for a large number of people, from skilled artisans and craftspeople to unskilled labor. The industry is an important source of income for many families and communities, providing economic opportunities and supporting local economies.

Materials and Pricing:

The production of jewelry in India is heavily influenced by the cost and availability of materials, including precious metals, gemstones, and diamonds. The pricing of jewelry is influenced by a range of factors, including the cost of materials, the labor involved in the production process, and the demand for specific pieces and styles.

Economic Impact:

The jewelry industry has a significant impact on the economy of India, contributing to economic growth and development, providing employment opportunities, and generating revenue through exports. The industry is also an important source of foreign currency, with jewelry exports accounting for a significant portion of the country's total exports.

The economics of Indian jewelry is a complex and dynamic field, with a rich history and tradition that continues to evolve and grow. Whether you are interested in the production process, the global market, or the impact of jewelry on the economy of India, "Adornments of India: A Journey Through the History and Artistry Behind Indian Jewelry" is an essential resource that provides a comprehensive overview of this fascinating and captivating industry.

"In India, jewelry is more than just an accessory, it is a celebration of life and the human spirit."

VII

The Cultural Significance of Indian Jewelry

Jewelry has played a significant role in the culture and traditions of India for thousands of years. From intricate gold and silver pieces to the use of precious gemstones, Indian jewelry is deeply rooted in the country's history, religion, and society. In this chapter, we will explore the cultural significance of Indian jewelry, including:

Religious Significance:

Jewelry is an important part of many religious traditions in India, with many pieces being used as offerings or gifts to the gods. Hinduism, for example, considers gold to be a symbol of purity and wealth, and it is often used in religious ceremonies and offerings. Similarly, in Buddhism, the use of jewelry is seen as a way to show respect for the gods and to express devotion.

Social Significance:

Jewelry is also an important part of the social fabric of India, with many pieces being used to symbolize social status, wealth, and beauty. Jewelry is often given as gifts to commemorate special events, such as weddings and anniversaries, and it is also a common way to express love and affection.

Aesthetic Significance:

Indian jewelry is renowned for its beauty and craftsmanship, with a rich history of design and tradition. The use of intricate patterns, intricate detailing, and the use of precious materials has made Indian jewelry a symbol of style and elegance, both in India and around the world.

Cultural Significance:

Indian jewelry is also a reflection of the country's rich cultural heritage, with many pieces being inspired by traditional stories, legends, and myths. For example, the intricate designs of Meenakari jewelry are inspired by the stories of Hindu gods and goddesses, while the use of gemstones in Indian jewelry is often linked to the country's astrological beliefs.

Political Significance:

Jewelry has also played a significant role in the politics of India, with many pieces being used as symbols of power and wealth. For example, the use of diamonds and precious gems in jewelry was often a symbol of the wealth and power of Indian royalty, with many pieces being used to signal their status and influence.

The cultural significance of Indian jewelry is a complex and fascinating subject, with a rich history and tradition that continues to evolve and grow. Whether you are interested in the religious, social, aesthetic, or political significance of Indian jewelry, "Adornments of India: A Journey Through the History and Artistry Behind Indian Jewelry" provides a comprehensive overview of this captivating and richly textured industry.

"*The intricate Meenakari enamel work of the Mughal era remains one of the most iconic and enduring styles in Indian jewelry.*"

સ

VIII

Impact of Indian Jewelry on Society

Jewelry has had a profound impact on Indian society and culture, influencing everything from economic and political systems to religious beliefs and fashion trends. In this chapter, we will explore the various ways that Indian jewelry has impacted society, including:

Economic Impact:

The jewelry industry has been a major source of employment and economic growth in India, with many families relying on the production and sale of jewelry as their primary source of income. Additionally, the jewelry industry has played a major role in attracting foreign investment, with many international companies setting up operations in India to take advantage of the country's rich tradition of jewelry making.

Social Impact:

Jewelry has played a significant role in shaping social norms and traditions in India, influencing everything from the way people express their love and affection to the way they express their cultural identity. For example, the use of jewelry as a symbol of wealth and social status has helped to create and reinforce a hierarchical social structure, while the use of jewelry as a symbol of religious devotion has helped to reinforce the country's strong spiritual and cultural traditions.

Political Impact:

Jewelry has also had a significant impact on politics in India, with many pieces being used to symbolize power, wealth, and status. For example, the use of diamonds and precious gems in jewelry has often been associated with political power, with many Indian rulers using their jewelry collections to signal their wealth and influence. Additionally, the jewelry industry has also been an important source of revenue for the Indian government, with taxes on jewelry sales helping to fund public services and infrastructure.

Cultural Impact:

The intricate and beautiful designs of Indian jewelry have had a major impact on the country's cultural landscape, inspiring new styles, trends, and fashions. The rich history and tradition of Indian jewelry making has helped to create a cultural identity that is unique and distinct, with many pieces being recognized and celebrated as symbols of

Indian heritage and cultural pride.

Environmental Impact:

The production of jewelry can have a significant impact on the environment, with many jewelry making processes involving the use of toxic chemicals and metals. However, in India, there is a growing movement towards sustainable and environmentally responsible jewelry production, with many artisan communities embracing new techniques and materials that are more sustainable and environmentally friendly.

The impact of Indian jewelry on society is a complex and multifaceted subject, with many different factors coming into play. Whether you are interested in the economic, social, political, cultural, or environmental impact of Indian jewelry, "Adornments of India: A Journey Through the History and Artistry Behind Indian Jewelry" provides a comprehensive overview of this fascinating and important industry.

"The Victorian styles and techniques introduced during the British Raj continue to inspire contemporary Indian jewelry design."

Indian Traditional Jewelry Set

IX

Indian Jewelry and the Global Market

The jewelry industry in India has been growing rapidly in recent years, with many Indian designers and manufacturers exporting their products to a growing global market. In this chapter, we will examine the role that Indian jewelry plays in the global market, including:

Export Market:

Indian jewelry has been a major contributor to the country's export market, with many Indian manufacturers exporting their products to other countries around the world. The main export destinations for Indian jewelry include the United States, the United Kingdom, and the Middle East, with these countries accounting for a large portion of India's total jewelry exports.

Competition in the Global Market:

Indian jewelry faces significant competition in the global market, with many countries around the world producing and exporting jewelry products. However, Indian jewelry has managed to maintain its competitiveness through a combination of factors, including the country's rich history and tradition of jewelry making, the high quality and craftsmanship of Indian jewelry, and the unique and distinctive styles and designs of Indian jewelry.

Impact on Local Artisans:

The growing export market for Indian jewelry has had a major impact on local artisans, with many communities relying on the production and sale of jewelry as their primary source of income. The export market has also provided many artisans with new opportunities and resources, allowing them to expand their businesses, increase their production, and improve the quality of their products.

Import Market:

In addition to its role in the export market, India also has a growing import market for jewelry, with many international companies setting up operations in the country to take advantage of the rich tradition of jewelry making and the high quality and craftsmanship of Indian jewelry. The main import markets for Indian jewelry include the United States, the United Kingdom, and Europe, with these countries accounting for a large portion of India's total jewelry imports.

Challenges in the Global Market:

Despite its many strengths, the Indian jewelry industry faces a number of challenges in the global market, including the high cost of raw materials, competition from other jewelry producing countries, and the limited resources and infrastructure available to many local artisans. To address these challenges, the Indian government and the jewelry industry have been working together to develop new strategies and programs to support the growth and development of the industry.

The impact of Indian jewelry on the global market is a complex and dynamic subject, with many different factors coming into play. Whether you are interested in the export market, the competition in the global market, the impact on local artisans, the import market, or the challenges faced by the Indian jewelry industry, "Adornments of India: A Journey Through the History and Artistry Behind Indian Jewelry" provides a comprehensive overview of this fascinating and important industry.

"Indian jewelry is a window into the country's rich history, reflecting its cultural and artistic achievements."

X

The Future of Indian Jewelry

The jewelry industry in India has a rich and dynamic history, and it continues to play a major role in the country's economy, culture, and society. Looking to the future, the Indian jewelry industry is poised for even greater growth and success, with many exciting new developments and trends emerging in the field. In this chapter, we will explore some of the key trends and challenges shaping the future of Indian jewelry, including:

Technological Innovations:

One of the most important trends shaping the future of Indian jewelry is the increasing use of new technologies and materials in the jewelry making process. From 3D printing to new alloys and synthetic materials, these technological innovations are changing the way that jewelry is designed, manufactured, and sold, offering new opportunities for creativity, efficiency, and affordability.

Growing Consumer Demand:

The demand for jewelry continues to grow both in India and around the world, with many consumers seeking out unique, high-quality pieces that reflect their personal style and values. As consumers become more conscious of the environmental and social impacts of their purchases, the demand for eco-friendly and ethically sourced jewelry is also expected to increase.

Increasing Competition:

The global jewelry market is becoming increasingly competitive, with many countries around the world producing and exporting jewelry products. To remain competitive in this global market, Indian jewelry manufacturers will need to continue to invest in new technologies and techniques, and focus on producing high-quality, distinctive products that appeal to consumers both in India and around the world.

Sustainability and Ethical Practices:

Another important trend shaping the future of Indian jewelry is the growing focus on sustainability and ethical practices in the industry. Consumers are becoming increasingly concerned about the environmental and social impacts of the products they purchase, and are seeking out jewelry that is produced in a sustainable and responsible manner.

The Rise of E-Commerce:

The rise of e-commerce has had a profound impact on the jewelry industry in India, providing consumers with greater access to a wider range of products and allowing manufacturers and retailers to reach new markets and customers. Looking to the future, the growth of e-commerce is expected to continue, offering new opportunities for innovation, growth, and success for the Indian jewelry industry.

The future of Indian jewelry is full of exciting possibilities, as the industry continues to evolve and adapt to meet the changing needs and expectations of consumers both in India and around the world. Whether you are a jewelry maker, designer, retailer, or consumer, "Adornments of India: A Journey Through the History and Artistry Behind Indian Jewelry" provides an in-depth look at the trends and challenges shaping the future of this fascinating and important industry.

"The legacy of Indian jewelry is a testament to the ingenuity and creativity of the country's master artisans."

☙

XI

The Legacy of Indian Jewelry

India has a rich and diverse history in the art of jewelry making, dating back to the Indus Valley Civilization (3300–1300 BCE). Jewelry was not only an adornment, but also held religious and cultural significance. The tradition of jewelry making has been passed down through generations and has been influenced by various cultures including the Mughals, the British, and the Portuguese. The result is a stunning and unique fusion of styles, designs, and techniques that define the legacy of Indian jewelry.

Indus Valley Civilization

The Indus Valley Civilization, one of the world's earliest civilizations, was renowned for its metalwork and jewelry making. Archaeologists have discovered a wealth of jewelry including necklaces, bracelets, earrings, and nose rings made of gold, silver, and bronze. These pieces were often decorated with intricate designs and precious stones such as carnelian and turquoise. Jewelry was an important aspect of daily life and held spiritual significance, with some pieces even believed to have served as talismans to ward off evil.

The Mughal Era

The Mughal Empire (1526–1857 CE) left a lasting impact on Indian jewelry, particularly in the form of enamel work, also known as Meenakari. The Mughals brought the technique of enameling from Persia, and it was further developed in India, incorporating the use of bright, vibrant colors. Jewelry was also decorated with precious and semi-precious stones, including diamonds, pearls, and emeralds. The Mughal emperors were known for their love of jewelry and commissioned the creation of magnificent pieces, often as gifts to their queens and concubines.

The British Raj

During the British Raj (1858–1947 CE), jewelry making in India was heavily influenced by Victorian styles and techniques. Jewelers adopted new methods and materials, including machine-made components and synthetic gems. Despite this, traditional techniques and designs still played a significant role in the creation of jewelry. One notable example is the Jadau jewelry of Rajasthan, which is still highly prized and sought after today.

Contemporary Indian Jewelry

Today, Indian jewelry continues to evolve and be influenced

by a wide range of styles and techniques. From traditional techniques like Meenakari, to modern techniques such as 3D printing, Indian jewelry is renowned for its beauty and craftsmanship. With the rise of e-commerce, Indian jewelry has gained a global following and is now more accessible than ever before.

The legacy of Indian jewelry is one that is rich and diverse, reflecting the country's history and cultural heritage. From the Indus Valley Civilization to the contemporary era, jewelry has been an integral part of life in India, holding both aesthetic and spiritual significance. Whether made using traditional techniques or modern methods, Indian jewelry continues to captivate and inspire.

"From the sparkling diamonds of Jaipur to the handcrafted gold of Kerala, Indian jewelry is a diverse and vibrant tapestry of styles and designs."

⚭

More Quotes on Indian Jewelry

"The contemporary Indian jewelry scene is a dynamic and ever-evolving landscape, reflecting the country's passion for beauty and craftsmanship."

"The legacy of Indian jewelry is a story of perseverance, passion, and artistic excellence, spanning centuries and civilizations."

"For generations, jewelry has been an essential part of daily life in India, a symbol of identity, status, and spiritual connection."

"In India, jewelry is not simply a thing of beauty, it is a celebration of the country's rich history and cultural heritage, a tribute to its enduring artistic traditions."

૪૭

OTHER BOOKS OF THE AUTHOR

1. The Moments When I Met God
2. Kashiyile Theertha Pathangal
3. GURU GYAN VANI
4. Abhiprerak Gita
5. ASSI SE JAIN GHAT TAK
6. Hopelessness of Arjuna
7. The Soul and It's True Nature
8. Sense of Action (Karma)
9. Action through Wisdom
10. Action through Wisdom
11. THEORY AND PRACTICAL OF EVERY ACTION
12. LOGICAL UNDERSTANDING OF THE SUPREME
13. THE IMPERISHABLE SUPREME
14. Yatra Nishadraj se Hanuman Ghat Tak
15. Yatra Karnatak Ghat se Raja Ghat Tak
16. Yatra Pandey Ghat se Prayagraj Ghat Tak
17. Yatra Ranjendra Prasad Ghat se Dattatreya Ghat Tak
18. YaatraSindhiya Ghat se Gwaliar Ghat Tak
19. Yatra Mangala Gauri Ghat se Hanuman Gadhi Ghat Tak
20. Yatra Gaay Ghat Se Nishad Ghat Tak
21. MAA GANGA, GHATEN EVM UTSAV
22. Ganga Arti Dev Deepavali evam Any Utsav
23. Potentials of Digitalized India
24. VEDIC CONSCIOUSNESS
25. A Brief Introduction to Vedic Science
26. Kashi ke Barah Jyotirling
27. IMPACT OF MOTIVATION
28. Let's have a Milky Way Journey
29. Color Therapy in a Nutshell

30. Rigveda in a Nutshell
31. Yajurveda in a Nutshell
32. Samveda in a Nutshell
33. Atharva Veda in a Nutshell
34. Ayushman Bhava - Ayurveda
35. Srimad Bhagavad Gita and Upanishad Connection
36. Srimad Bhagavad Gita - an attempt to summarize each chapter.
37. Facts and Impact of Nakshatra
38. Astro Gems - NAVARATNA
39. Ekadashi - A Concise Overview
40. A Concise View of Hanuman Chalisa
41. Inspirational Gita
42. Nakshatraranyam
43. Summary of 18 Mahapuranas
44. Synopsis of 18 Upa Puranas
45. Rigvediya Upanishads
46. Shukla Yajurvediya Upanishads
47. Krishna Yajurvediya Upanishads
48. Samavediya Upanishads
49. Atharvavediya Upanishads
50. The Seven Great Sages
51. From Rocket Scientist to President Dr. APJ Abdul Kalam
52. The Visionary's Voice - Quotes of Dr. APJ Abdul Kalam
53. The Wisdom of Swami Vivekananda: Insights and Inspiration from a Legendary Spiritual Teacher
54. Ayurvedic Remedies from the Garden
55. Sages and Seers
56. Rising Strong – Motivational Stories of Women
57. Beyond Flames -Mystery stories of Funeral Ghat Manikarnika
58. The Origins of Tulsi: A Look at the Mythological Roots of the Plant"

59. The Holistic Cow: A Look at the Physical, Spiritual, and Cultural Importance of Cows in India
60. Arts of Healing
61. Exploring the Divine
62. Understanding Five Elements
63. The Etymology of Ram
64. Symbols of India
65. Voice of Change (About Speeches of Great Men)
66. She Speaks (About Speeches of Great Women)
67. Patriotism on Celluloid – Brief About Patriotic Films
68. The Music of Motivation: A Brief Guide to Inspirational Film Songs
69. Unlocking the Secrets of the Dashopanishads
70. A Cultural Mosaic
71. Ancient Traditions, Modern Minds
72. Ecos of Ancient Wisdom
73. Beneath the Surface
74. From Temples to Ashrams
75. Sages of the Subcontinent
76. The Art of Healling (Ayurveda, Yoga & Naturopathy)
77. Indian Kitchen
78. The Festivals of India
79. The Indian Epics Retold
80. The Power of Mantras
81. The Indian River Ganges
82. The Indian Architecture
83. Rites of Passage
84. The Indian Silk Road
85. The Indian Literature
86. The Indian Villages
87. The Indian Folks & Crafts
88. The Way of Buddha
89. The Ramayan of Tulsidas

CONTACT

DR. JAGADEESH PILLAI

MBA & PhD in Vedic Science

Four Times Guinness World Record Holder

Winner of Mahatma Gandhi Vishwa Shanti Puraskar and
Global Peace Ambassador

Gemology, Astro & Vastu Consultant - Spiritual Counselor

Consultant for designing World Record Ideas

Efficient Tarot Card Reader

9839093003

myrichindia@gmail.com

drjagadeeshpillai@facebook

drjagadeeshpillai@instagram

jagadeeshpillai@youtube

www. JAGADEESHPILLAI.com

ॐ

|| LOKAHA SAMASTHAHA SUKHINO BHAVANTU ||

www.ingramcontent.com/pod-product-compliance
Lightning Source LLC
Chambersburg PA
CBHW021115130726
47988CB00003B/1037